Dear Parents,

Children's earliest experiences with stories and books usually involve grown-ups reading to them. However, reading should be active, and as adults, we can help young readers make meaning of the text by prompting them to relate the book to what they already know and to their personal experiences. Our questions will lead them to move beyond the simple story and pictures and encourage them to think beneath the surface. For example, after reading a story about the sleep habits of animals, you might ask, "Do you remember when you moved into a big bed? Could you see the moon out of your window?"

Illustrations in these books are wonderful and can be used in a variety of ways. Your questions about them can direct the child to details and encourage him or her to think about what those details tell us about the story. You might ask the child to find three different "beds" used by animals and insects in the book. Illustrations can even be used to inspire readers to draw their own pictures related to the text.

At the end of each book, there are some suggested questions and activities related to the story. These questions range in difficulty and will help you move young readers from the text itself to thinking skills such as comparing and contrasting, predicting, applying what they learned to new situations and identifying things they want to find out more about. This conversation about their reading may even result in the children becoming the storytellers, rather than simply the listeners!

Harriet Ziefert, M.A.
Language Arts/Reading Specialist

More to  About

Does a Bear Wear Boots?

Does a Beaver Sleep in a Bed?

Does a Camel Cook Spaghetti?

Does a Hippo Go to the Doctor?

Does a Panda Go to School?

Does a Seal Smile?

Does a Tiger Go to the Dentist?

Does a Woodpecker Use a Hammer?

Think  About how everyone sees

Does an Owl Wear Eyeglasses?

Harriet Ziefert • illustrations by Emily Bolam

BLUE APPLE

Text copyright © 2014, 2023 by Harriet Ziefert
Illustrations copyright © 2014, 2023 by Emily Bolam
All rights reserved
CIP data is available.
First published in the United States 2014 by
🍎 Blue Apple Books
South Orange, New Jersey

Does an owl wear eyeglasses?

No! You must be joking.
An owl never wears eyeglasses.

An owl has poor day vision and excellent night vision.
If it sees a mouse on the ground, it follows it for a while.
Then it swoops down for a mouse dinner. Ugh!

Does a goat wear eyeglasses?

How silly! A goat in eyeglasses? Never!
A goat eating eyeglasses? Maybe!

Goats have rectangular pupils, instead of round ones.
Most goats have brown eyes, but some have yellow.
Goats see better at night than people,
and sometimes find food when it's quite dark.

(Note: The pupil is the round, black part at the center of your eye.)

Does a butterfly fish wear eyeglasses?

Impossible!
Butterfly fish have two eyes on their face and
two fake eyes on their back end.
This confuses bigger fish who want to eat them.

Does a scallop wear eyeglasses?

Oh, no!
A scallop has 100 blue eyes.
Imagine 50 pair of glasses on a scallop!

Scallops can only see things that swim by slowly.
Then they catch and eat the food.
If anything goes by quickly, the scallop cannot see it.

Does an earthworm wear eyeglasses?

For goodness sake, no!
Eyeglasses need a nose to "sit on" and ears to wrap around.

Worms don't really have eyes.
But they have eye spots all over their bodies.
This is so they can tell light from dark.

Does a monkey wear eyeglasses?
Could be, but the answer is still no.

Monkeys have ears. Monkeys have a nose.
Monkeys use their eyes like people do.
Their eyesight has to be good.
A monkey with poor vision can't jump from branch
to branch. Or find nuts and fruits to eat.

What happens if a monkey is born with bad eyesight?

A monkey with poor eyesight cannot find food
and becomes small and weak.
It might slip and fall while swinging from tree to tree.

What happens when a child says:

A parent makes an appointment with an eye doctor. A doctor who specializes in eyes is called an *ophthalmologist*.

An ophthalmologist knows how to examine eyes.

An ophthalmologist know how to write a prescription for eyeglasses.

The right prescription gives good vision.
Good enough for seeing the TV, the blackboard,
for reading a book, signs . . . anything!

People wear all kinds of glasses.

sunglasses
(for protection
against the sun's rays)

goggles
(for seeing underwater,
swimming)

ski goggles
(for protection from wind and sun)

welder's glasses
(to protect eyes from the light of a welding torch)

motorcycle glasses
(for protection from wind and road dirt)

Some people are blind, and eyeglasses cannot help them see.
Many of these people use seeing eye dogs
to help them get around in the world.
They learn to read Braille.

Other people have vision
that cannot be corrected with eyeglasses.
These people use magnifying glasses. Or tablets.
The light from behind the screen helps them see the words.

People have invented things
other than eyeglasses to help vision:

magnifying glasses

Lots of people wear eyeglasses.
Does someone in your family wear eyeglasses?
Do you have a friend who wears eyeglasses?

Do you?

Think About how everyone sees

This book compares the eyesight of owls, goats, fish, worms, and monkeys to the way people see and correct their vision.

Compare and Contrast

- What animals have night vision? What animals have day vision? Compare and contrast how they live.

- What does it mean to be near-sighted or far-sighted? In the room you are in, what objects would you see best if you were near-sighted? How about far-sighted?

Braille is a language that allows visually impaired people to read.

- Find a braille book in a library. How is it different from reading a regular book?

Research

Go to a library or online to find out:

- What animals are nocturnal (animals that are awake at night)? What can you learn about how they see in the dark?

Bats are nocturnal and do not have good eyesight.

- How do they fly through the air and not bump into things?

People with blindness do amazing things and have made many discoveries.

- Choose a picture book biography about a blind person and read it.

Observe

Sight is just one of 5 senses. Close your eyes and use your other senses.

- What do you hear, smell, feel, or taste that tells you about the space around you? Try this inside and outside.

Many people wear eyeglasses to help them see better.

- Some take their eyeglasses on and off. Why do you think they do this?

Pets are using their eyesight all the time.

- When do they focus their eyes on humans?

Use a magnifying glass to look at things outdoors.

- What do you see that you had not noticed before?

Write, Tell, or Draw

Imagine a day with no sight.

- If you are able to see, imagine a day when you had to use all your other senses to get from your house to the end of your block. Draw a map of what you could smell, hear, or touch along the way.

What are your favorite sights?

- Make a list of the things you like to look at the most. Divide that list up into people, places, and things!

Draw all kinds of eyeglasses. Draw yourself in your favorite pair.

www.ingramcontent.com/pod-product-compliance
Lightning Source LLC
LaVergne TN
LVHW070837080426
835510LV00026B/3429